It's Circle Time!
Shapes

◾SCHOLASTIC

Children's Press®
A Division of Scholastic Inc.
New York Toronto London Auckland Sydney Mexico City
New Delhi Hong Kong Danbury, Connecticut

**Early Childhood
Consultants:**

**Ellen Booth Church
Diane Ohanesian**

1 2 3 4 5 6 7 8 9 10 R 19 18 17 16 15 14 13 12 11 10   62

Library of Congress Cataloging-in-Publication Data

Bolam, Emily.
  It's circle time! shapes / Emily Bolam.
      p. cm.
    ISBN-13: 978-0-531-24401-2 (lib. bdg.)   ISBN-13: 978-0-531-24576-7 (pbk.)
    ISBN-10: 0-531-24401-6 (lib. bdg.)   ISBN-10: 0-531-24576-4 (pbk.)
    1. Shapes – Juvenile literature. I. Title.

  QA445.5.P46 2009
  516'.15 – dc22   2009004773

It's circle time!

It's time to play
with shapes we see most every day!

We made **circles**.
1, 2, 3!

Look around and you will see.

Circles hanging on the walls.
Circles in the shape of balls.

Find the circles in a tree.
Find the circle on a knee.

We made **squares.**

It's so much **fun!**

Look around. Find more than one.

Red squares.
Green squares. Yellow, too!

There's a square that's red and blue.

Find a square we like to eat.
Find a square on the red seat.

We made **triangles**.
Big and small.

Look around and find them all.

Triangles on doors.
Triangle boats.

Triangle flags.
Triangles on coats!

14

Find the triangle
that is a hat.

Find a blue triangle
on the mat.

We made **rectangles.**
Here and there.

Look around. They're everywhere!

One rectangle on the floor.
One rectangle is the door!

Find a rectangle
that's big and red.
It's pillowy soft to lay your head.

Circle time is so much fun,

20

when shapes go marching one by one.

21

Shapes are

Circle

Triangle

marching everywhere...

Rectangle

Square

Rookie Storytime Tips

It's Circle Time! Shapes is a lively introduction to basic shapes. As you enjoy this book with your child, encourage him or her to find and point to as many examples of each shape as possible on each page. You'll be building the important preschool skill of shape recognition.

Invite your preschooler to go back and find the following. As your child explores the book again, he or she will build visual discrimination and reinforce additional preschool skills.

Can you find more green triangles?

What else is hanging on the classroom wall?

What do you eat that's shaped like a square?

Ask your child to look around the room you're in. Can he or she find a circle? A triangle? What other shapes does he or she see?